Fearlessly Frugal

Learn how to live happier and healthier for less

PAUL MORRISEY

Copyright © 2016 Paul Morrisey

All rights reserved. No part of this publication may be reproduced or transmitted in any form or by any means, mechanical or electronic, including photocopying or recording, or by any information storage and retrieval system, or transmitted by email without the permission in writing from the publisher.

ISBN:1539303942

ISBN-13:9781539303947

Your Free Gift

I want to show my appreciation for your support, so I've put together a free gift for you.

In Habit Stacking for Success, you'll discover a variety if tips, tricks, and routines that you can use to effectively build good habits that will make your life better. You will learn how to be more efficient and productive in all aspects of your life.

www.EverGreenLearner.com/mybonus

Just visit the link above to download it now.

I know you will get a lot out of it, especially if you read this book first!

Thanks!

Paul Morrisey

CONTENTS

Introduction	6
What's the point of a frugal lifestyle	9
Strive to be debt-free	14
Your things don't own you	18
It's all just stuff…	23
A Fresh Start	28
Budgeting	33
Tips, Tricks & Sneaky Ways to Find More Money	39
Conclusion	53

Introduction

> "If we did the things we are capable of doing, we would literally astound ourselves."
>
> -Thomas Edison

Frugal living is about much more than just saving money. It's about enjoying a better life with fewer 'things,' planning for a more secure future and making your life simpler, but better. Today, more than ever, people are embracing frugal living, not because they can't afford a luxurious lifestyle, but because living simply is becoming a more attractive lifestyle option than living beyond your means.

More people are beginning to understand the value of saving money and spending less. It's a concept that makes great sense, not just in the present, but in the future as well. If you live beyond your means today, you'll only have debt to look forward to when you retire. However, by choosing to make a few small sacrifices today, you can look forward to a retirement that's not only more financially secure, but that will allow you to live the type of life you want..

Frugal living doesn't require genius math skills or monk-like self-sacrifice, although it does help if you can work a budget like a ninja and don't mind passing up a few little luxuries along the way. In fact, the most successful frugal living is done by taking baby steps, making small changes that add up, and changing the way you feel about your money and your 'stuff.'

Most people probably think of living frugally as living a lifestyle that denies you any gratification or luxury, but that's pretty far from the truth. Instead, it's a way of life that teaches you to enjoy more of what you currently have, learn to live on less money and adopt an approach that results in delayed gratification that is even sweeter than you could imagine.

If you want to go on a little adventure, one in which the destination is more important and exciting than the journey itself, read on. In this guide to living frugally, you'll find out that frugal living can be fun, freeing and incredibly rewarding. Plus, it's not half as challenging as you might expect it to be. You'll learn how to make the most of what you already have, figure out how to create a budget that meets YOUR needs, plan for a financially secure future and embrace an attitude of self-sufficiency.

Start your journey to frugal living right now, so you can enjoy your debt-free destination as soon as possible!

What's the point of a frugal lifestyle

"People buy things they don't need, with money they don't have, to impress people they don't like."

– Clive Hamilton

If the thought of saving money seems like a foreign concept to you, you're not alone. Today's society seems to encourage more a 'buy now, worry about it later' attitude when it comes to money, so it's no wonder that so many of us are dragging around debt. It seems okay to be broke, living paycheck to paycheck, or toting around huge car payments, mortgages and credit card balances. It's what everyone else does, so why should you be any different, right?

Well, for a start, today isn't going to last forever. Time marches on, and as you age, if you still have lots of debt to pay off, it's going to be pretty difficult to do that when you retire and have less money coming in. In fact, if you are in a lot of debt, retirement might not even be possible.

Think about the kind of future you want. Most of us want to retire with enough money in the bank to know that our bills will be paid and that we can travel a little, maybe visit friends and family. We want to enjoy retirement by doing things, not necessarily having them. Unfortunately, while you're young and earning money, most people have a strong desire to 'have' things instead. This mindset means that most of us live beyond our means, trying to keep up with everyone else, always buying the latest and greatest of whatever society is selling us.

It's unfortunate that during the most productive years of our lives financially, many of us take on debt or neglect to save money for those years when our income is very low or non-existent. Consider two people, let's call them Bob and Jim.

Bob worked hard and lived within his means. While he spent money on things that mattered to him, there was always a budget and a long-term financial goal in mind. Now he is retired, Bob is reaping the benefits of his frugal lifestyle by not having to worry about bills, money or work.

Jim is also retired, but unlike Bob, Jim was not a great saver. Jim struggles to make ends meet, and while he is managing, it is not the retirement he always thought he would enjoy. He is still worried about money.

Who would you rather be?

Now, this book isn't written to tell you how to invest your money wisely so you'll be like that active, probably wealthy retiree mentioned first. Instead, think of it as a tool that you can use to help figure out ways to free up money to invest in your future. Later in the book, you'll find tips on various means to save money, find 'hidden' money you probably don't realize was there and stretch your money further so you can live better for less.

If you're one of those people who just can't think that far ahead, and who can't envision how your retired life will look, consider this instead. Do you currently live paycheck to paycheck? Are you one disaster away from financial ruin? For many people, the answer to both of these is 'yes.' Do you have enough savings to cover your expenses if you fall sick? How long would you last, one week? One month? Three months? Would losing your job also trigger losing your car or your home because you can't keep up with the payments?

It's scary to think about these things, and that's probably why most people don't. They just keep plugging on, spending money and trying to keep up with everyone else, without saving a penny for those types of emergencies. Frugal living isn't even a consideration for these people because everything is fine as long as they keep working and bringing in money.

Some people know that frugal living could be

a better option, but they aren't willing to try it because it seems either too restrictive or too difficult. They don't want to be broke for the rest of their lives, but they aren't willing to make the necessary changes to break the cycle and secure a better future for themselves. They want their cake, and they want to eat every bit of it.

The problem with both of these mindsets is that they leave you financially vulnerable, both now and in the future. Making a small change in your mindset can have a huge impact on your wallet, and it's not as difficult as you might think.

If you still aren't sure how a frugal lifestyle could benefit you beyond giving you a more financially secure retirement, consider these other benefits.

1. You'll be healthier.

If you get your finances in check and have savings to fall back on, your stress levels will plummet. Less stress means lower risks of heart attacks and strokes, plus you'll feel better. And if you spend less money on unhealthy fast foods and processed junk, you'll probably see a difference in your energy levels and waistline.

2. You'll feel happier.

Less worrying about money means less arguing about it with your spouse, or the debt collectors. In fact, when not focused on how much money you don't have, you begin to appreciate the things that you do have. The newfound sense of gratitude will help make you feel amazing.

3. You will gain confidence.

Once you master the art of telling your money what to do, there will be no stopping you. Seriously, tackling your debt, and winning, is one of the best ways to feel better about your life. You'll feel more in control and hopefully you'll continue to make healthy choices for the rest of your life.

The next chapter will go into more detail about the benefits of frugal living, but I think you get the general idea. It's a good thing, and it's not hard to do.

You don't have to follow the crowd when it comes to money. Frugal living can seem like a strange concept, but it doesn't have to. In fact, frugal living doesn't mean living in poverty. It does mean making some changes now so that you can enjoy life more in the longer term.

Strive to be debt-free

> "The most important rule in achieving your goals…is that distracting opportunities have to die for your most important goals to live."
>
> – Aaron Dignan, from *Manage Your Day to Day*

'Okay,' you say, 'I get that saving money is good, but the future is a long way off, and I want to enjoy my life. Why should I worry about living frugally now when I can just double up on my efforts later on?' Well, for a start, tomorrow's not a given, and there's no guarantee that you'll be in a position to play 'catch-up' later on.

Before you decide that frugal living involves too much effort for goals that are long term, take a minute to think about what you want out of life. If you're like most people, you probably want to travel more, have nicer things, spend more time with your friends and family, and probably spend a good chunk of time sitting by the pool sipping fruity drinks with a good book in hand. You get the picture.

Of course, you could have all those things right now if you have access to enough cash or credit. If you spend all your money today on these things, and tomorrow you lose your job, at least you'll have your cool new car and memories of all those trips to keep you warm and fed, right? If you happened to be hurt or get sick and can't work anymore, not only do you have to cover your living expenses now, but you'll also have to have money to live on for the rest of your life. Unless you want to live in abject poverty off of government 'assistance,' it only makes good sense to get your ducks in a row financially while you're young and able.

There are a few more reasons why you should consider getting out of debt, and they have very little to do with planning for your future. In today's 'stuff' troubled world, it can be truly difficult to feel satisfied, especially if you try to keep up with everyone around you. There's always something new and great that you just 'need,' but do you really need it?

It's very easy to fall into the trap of feeling somehow 'less than' if you can't afford the finer things in life. It's also very easy to forget to be grateful for the things you do have. This attitude leads to lots of feeling sorry for yourself, which can even trigger depression. A lack of gratitude can have an overall negative impact on your emotions and your life in general.

Even if you are grateful for the things you

have, you can still suffer from negative feelings if you live a lifestyle that's beyond your means or you don't prepare yourself financially for emergencies. Have you ever reached a point where your money just ran out, but you still had days or even weeks to go before you get paid again? That's a very stressful situation to find yourself in, but it's more common than you might think.

The stress and anxiety of not having enough money in your savings to cover your basic living costs can be overwhelming, especially if you have a family to support. If you have credit cards, you may feel like it's a good idea just to pay for these costs with credit, but that just makes the problem worse by deepening your debt.

It's a common myth that only people who spend money foolishly are in debt. You can live a relatively modest lifestyle, but still be in debt, if you don't learn to manage your money. Frugal living can help you do just that, and more. It can help you plan for the future, so you won't have to worry about where you'll find the money to cover your living expenses once you retire. It can also help you feel more satisfied with your life now, teaching you to appreciate living on less money. It can help free you from those feelings of anxiety, because you'll feel more in control of your money, and it can obliterate that stress you get every month when the money's all gone, but you still have bills to pay and mouths to feed.

Eliminating debt can make you feel more financially secure, and it can bust the stress of having to face those weeks where the money runs out before the month does. Less money stress means less arguing with your partner about money, and it also means that the money you bring into your home YOURS, and not your debt collectors. You can spend wisely, by living frugally, and put money away in your savings account so that you can look forward to a bright future.

Once you break the debt cycle and begin to use your money for your individual needs, you can choose to spend your money in ways that are meaningful to you, whether that's spending more time with your family, donating to charity or just making sure that your family lives a healthy, happy lifestyle.

Debt may be familiar, but that doesn't mean it has to be your 'normal.' Buck the trend, embrace frugal living, and ditch your debt for a better life today and tomorrow.

Your things don't own you

"A journey of a thousand *ri* proceeds step by step."

– Lao Tze, from *the Tao Te Ching*

When it's all said and done, the stuff you buy is just 'stuff.' It doesn't define you; it doesn't make you a better person, and it doesn't have to limit you. If the things we own don't do these things, why do we keep buying so much of it?

Human beings have a nasty habit of judging each other by the way they look, live or act. If you look poor, lack the latest fashions or technology and generally don't spend money, there's a stigma attached to you. It just isn't normal to not spend money, but it should be.

You can't change the fact that people are going to look at you and your lifestyle and make judgments. However, you can change how you react to these judgments. In the words of a certain pop-star, 'shake it off.' Learn to care less about what other people think, and more about how you'll feel once you're debt-free, and you will be able to embrace and even enjoy living frugally like you never thought you would.

Look at your belongings for what they really are: objects that either serve a purpose, make you feel good, or that just look pretty and take up space in your home. If you have items that fall into the last category, consider whether or not you need them. Wouldn't you love to get rid of some of that clutter? Wouldn't life be simpler if you didn't have those things sitting around, taking up space?

When you choose to live a materialistic lifestyle, it sets off a never-ending cycle of disappointment. You buy the latest and greatest 'thing,' and within a few weeks, it's outdated, so you start to envy people buying the newer versions. You see this all the time with cell phones and cars, and most people don't even realize that smart brand marketing is getting the better of them. Those big brand names spend a lot of time and money on marketing because they understand your human nature better than you do: everyone wants to feel like they are the best.

Being the best often means having the best, so you feel like you must buy bigger and better stuff to make up for the fact that the first stuff you bought is old and not-so-shiny anymore. In marketing, this is called Shiny Object Syndrome, and you can believe that marketers love people who suffer from this!

Of course, having stuff isn't all bad. Some things, like a home and clothes, you need. But, do you need the most expensive designer clothes? Do you need the house with 5000 square feet of space? If you can learn to differentiate your needs from your wants, you will have almost won the debt battle. Too many times, you buy things based on emotions and desires rather than your actual needs, and then you feel guilty about it.

If you can learn to separate your emotions when making purchases, you'll almost always come up buying the most cost efficient item for your needs. But, this is easier said than done and takes a lot of conscious effort on your part, so most people just rely on soothing those same old emotional needs through retail therapy.

If you can dare to be different, you will learn that only buying what you need right now means that later on you can afford to buy the things you want, and you'll appreciate them more because you had to wait for them.

If the idea of thinking this way, of thinking differently from everyone else around you, scares you, it's okay. Knowledge is powerful stuff, and once you know how to buy things based on your needs rather than your desires, you'll be ahead of everyone else in the race to financial freedom. You may have to make the choice and be brave enough to be different from the masses of debt-laden zombies who are spending their way into an eternity of being broke. Or, you could try and 'wake up' your friends and family who still feel that they have to buy stuff to make themselves feel important or happy.

How can you reach the point where you are detached from what you buy? How can you tell if you're buying something because you need it, or because you want it? It can be tricky, but you can use these tips to help you decide.

- Is the item something you need to stay alive, like shelter, food or clothing?

- Is there a cheaper version or alternative that you could buy that would meet your needs as well?

- If you don't have the money to pay for the item, can it wait a few days or weeks until you save up the cash? (Hint: If the answer is 'yes,' it's probably more of a want than a need.)

- Are you buying the item because it's on sale, and you think you might need it in

> future? (While this may sound like a good idea, buying something because it's cheap isn't saving money, it's justifying spending. Unless it is something that you truly will use and would have bought nonetheless.)

You have to realize that you live in a world that is always happy to tell you what they think you need. If you want to be clever with your money, you stop letting others tell you how to spend it. If you believe that you aren't letting other people guide your purchases, just ask yourself why you want that certain new thing that you've got your heart set on. Is it because you need it to make your life better, or is it because you'll look cool using it and it will impress other people?

Once you realize that you are defined by what you buy or own, you become free to make better choices that will help you achieve your ultimate financial freedom.

It's all just stuff...

"You know my methods. Apply them!"

– Sherlock Holmes

You probably had a favorite toy or two when you were a child, something that made you smile and comforted you when you were sad. As you outgrew toys, you probably developed sentimental attachments to other things, like favorite articles of clothing, favorite albums (or CD's), or other items that held some emotional significance.

Once you left home and became independent, you probably became quite fond of the 'stuff' you accumulated because it represented the fact that you were now independent and 'grown-up.' Even if you didn't develop a deep and passionate love for, say, your first refrigerator, you probably were pretty excited to buy it, because it represented something that you wanted to be: an independent adult who was no longer reliant on others for support.

You may not think that you are emotionally attached to the things you buy, but if you're like most people, you're probably way more connected than you realize. If you were asked to go through your home and pick out the things that you couldn't live without, it would probably be easy. You would probably pick out the necessities first, then a few items that held high sentimental value, like photographs or gifts that you've received.

Do you really need it?

Now, if you were asked to take a look at everything in your home and seek out a cheaper alternative, how many of those 'necessities' would you be willing to trade for a different model? Sometimes, we buy things both because we need them and because we want them. This approach makes it harder to tell if we're buying them because they are necessities, or because they are cooler versions of the things we need. If you can afford the more expensive version of something and you still have savings in the bank, you might be okay buying that more expensive item, but do you need it? Would the cheaper version work as well, without jeopardizing your finances?

If you're reading this book, you probably don't have the cash to buy the more expensive item, and you probably don't have any money in your savings account, so it's most likely that the item is a 'want' version of something you need. For example, if you are a writer, and you need a new computer because your old one has stopped working, you may want a touch screen computer because they are new and fresh and very fun to use.

However, they are also much more expensive, in most cases, than a traditional computer without a touchscreen, and they don't do anything more or better than a traditional computer does. In this example, a touchscreen computer is more of a want than a need, and its extra cost could put you in a bind financially.

Eliminate emotion when making a purchase

When you make a purchase, you need to do so with clinical precision, if you ever want to be financially free. This commitment to purchasing without emotion is part of what frugal living is about, though it also encompasses many other techniques used to save money. You have to learn to look at every purchase based on facts, not on how owning the object will make you feel.

It's not hard to see how some people become addicted to shopping. Buying things that make you happy is fun, but it's not practical. If you've ever gone shopping and bought something because you felt that it would make you happy, then got home and had buyer's remorse when the credit card bill came, you'll know the power that 'stuff' has over some people. Owning things that make you feel good or that make you appear cool or important triggers some pretty strong emotions, but if you want to be debt free and financially independent, you need to learn to separate your 'stuff' from your emotions.

Look around your home. How much of what you own could be sold to pay off your debt or build a savings nest egg for your future retirement? How much of it do you need, and how much are you just holding onto because it makes you feel secure about who you are? Once you realize how strongly you are connected to these objects, you can begin to break those emotional bonds and recognize the objects for what they are.

At the end of the day, everything you own is just 'stuff.' It can't make your life better; it doesn't define who you are as a person, and it can't make you happy. Relationships with other people can provide these things, but your stuff cannot. It's not easy to do, but if you can become completely emotionally detached from the 'stuff' in your life, you can control your spending, learn to save more money and build a financial future that is secure and bright.

A Fresh Start

Before you ever even think about using frugal living to get yourself out of debt, you need to make sure you are in the right frame of mind. It's not a temporary solution. If you reduce your spending now, then go back to spending beyond your means once you've eliminated your debt, you'll probably end up back in debt, and find yourself facing the same situation you were in before.

You also have to look at the changes that you are making and think of it as starting fresh. Yes, you will need to make some sacrifices now, but think about all the benefits you'll reap from it. Think of how amazing it will feel to bring home a pay check that doesn't all go on paying off your debts? Imagine what life will be like when you have no car payment, no credit card debt, or even no mortgage payment every month? Think of all the great things your income can do for you when it belongs JUST to you.

Fight the fear, find financial freedom

You may be putting off making the changes necessary to get out of debt because they feel scary and like too much work, but think about how you feel every time you have to pay a credit card bill or loan payment. Think about how you feel when the week lasts longer than your paycheck, and you can't quite figure out which bill to pay first and which to let run overdue. Those feelings of anxiety over not having enough money are way worse than any minor discomforts you'll feel when you begin living frugally.

For some people, it can help to make a list of the things that they'd like to have or achieve once they are debt-free. List any financial price attached to these things, then look at one small habit or regular purchase that you could sacrifice to save for those things.

- Could you give up that pricey gourmet coffee from the coffee shop, or reduce the number of times you buy one each week?

- Could you take a lunch to work every day instead of eating fast food?

- Could you stop smoking, or cut back, to help save for your dream purchase? (This would save you money in health costs, too!)

There are probably dozens of small ways you could reduce your spending every week to put money towards getting out of debt or saving for a dream purchase. Many of these expenses seem so small that you might be tempted to think they don't make a big difference, but they do. If you drink five-$5 coffees every week, over the course of a year that equals $1300.

If you make a few small sacrifices every week, you probably won't miss the things you give up that much. Just make sure you replace them with free or low-cost alternatives, and you won't even feel deprived. For example, make yourself a cup of flavored coffee at home instead of buying from the coffee shop, cook tasty meals to take to work, etc. Most little luxuries have a cheaper or free alternative if you are willing to look for them.

Keeping a positive outlook is crucial to successful frugal living. If you go around telling yourself that you're being deprived, you'll just give into self-pity and fall off the wagon, slipping into the same bad habits that got you into debt in the first place. Staying positive means finding ways to appreciate the things you have when you are choosing to have less, and it means reminding yourself that the outcome is worth any temporary discomfort you feel that you might be experiencing. In other words, the struggle won't last forever, and if you stick with it, frugal living could be the most rewarding way to live your life because you will look forward to a great financial future.

Learning to say goodbye to old spending habits may be difficult, but it's not impossible, and it signifies the beginning of a new start to your finances. Once you can get past the feelings of 'woe is me,' you'll probably start to realize how lucky you are. After all, people in third world countries aren't complaining about having to give up a latte so they can afford to retire comfortably, so it may help to keep your 'sacrifices' in perspective.

And whenever you're tempted to feel jealous of your friends and family who are still living the high life, eating out every other night and spending way more money than you, just remember that you only see a tiny piece of their overall picture. They may have once been where you are now, but made their own sacrifices and are now enjoying the fruits of their efforts.

Or, they could be heading down the rabbit hole you just started clawing your way out of, financing their lifestyle with credit cards that will have to be paid off sooner or later. Who knows, maybe they'll see the changes that you are making in your life and commit to making some of their own. You could be the catalyst that helps others get their financial lives back on track, and that is hugely satisfying and very cool.

Squash the jealous feelings, kick the fears and doubts to the curb, and set your mind on success. A clean-slate state of mind will help you laser in on achieving your financial goals and meet them head on, so you can plan an awesome future.

Budgeting

If your eyes glaze over every time you hear the word 'budget,' you probably don't have a handle on your money. Budgets get a bad rap because they aren't the boring, drudge-filled documents that most people think they are. They're magical, beautiful things that put you back in control of your finances, but only if you stick to them.

There are lots of different budgeting methods you can use, but some are more effective than others. A budget is just a plan for your money, every penny of it. By telling your money where it needs to go every month, you can make sure that you stay in control of your finances.

Budgeting isn't difficult, but it may take you a few months to get used to making a budget that works for your needs. You need to know how much you earn, so you'll know what you can afford to allocate for everything you put on your budget. What goes on a budget? Anything you plan on spending money on, including your impulse purchases.

Look at what money you'll need to spend

during your next pay period. Don't wait until payday to do this; look at what you received on your last paycheck and use that as a guide. If you know you'll bring home, say $500, for example, and you know you have a $300 car payment due plus you need to buy groceries, you'll need to budget for both of those. You can't spend more than $200 on groceries, because of the car payment, so pick an amount that is practical.

Obviously, this is just an example, because real life never breaks down that smoothly. More than likely, you'll have some weeks where you have more bills than income, and others where you have more money than bills. The goal is to spread out that 'excess' money to cover those weeks where you really need it. Ideally, you'll also have a category for unexpected expenses.

If you have money left over in your budget, assign it a job. Savings is the most practical choice because it's good to have a safety net should an emergency pop up. But you also need to plan ahead for larger, predictable expenses, like auto insurance, taxes, and even Christmas shopping.

You can't fall into the trap of thinking that just because you have money left over in your checking account after you have paid your bills, you can spend that money willy-nilly. You need to realize that you need to plan ahead for those larger expenses and unexpected expenses, too. If you'd like to be able just to spend whenever you want on whatever you want, create a budget item for it. Set yourself a budget of $X.XX every pay period just for impulse spending, and spend it without feeling guilty, as long as you've budgeted all your necessities, too.

The beauty of budgeting is that it eliminates any nasty surprises if you do it right. If your car breaks down unexpectedly, but you have been planning ahead and putting away money every pay period for car repairs, you don't have to panic and put it on a credit card, digging your debt hole even deeper.

If you're wondering how you can keep track of every dollar you spend, you are in luck, because thanks to this wondrous age of technology that we live in, there are several great apps and pieces of software that make budgeting painless and even a little fun.

YNAB (You Need a Budget)

YNAB is a very popular piece of paid software that makes budgeting super simple. It stands for 'you need a budget,' and its principles are simple. First, you have to give every dollar you have a 'job.' Then, you have to make sure that you are including those long-term, larger expenses in your budgeting plans. (Sound familiar so far? It's the basis of any reliable budget!).

Once you know where your money needs to go, you can learn to make small adjustments, giving yourself permission to mess up now and then, but in a controlled way. At the end of the day, budgeting is just controlled chaos, because every single person budgets for different things, and you may not budget the same way from month to month or even week to week. It's okay to make changes to your budget by moving money from one budget category to another; it's not okay to overspend every month and fall back on your credit cards.

The Envelope System

Another tried, and true method of budgeting is the envelope system. Lots of people use this system--in fact, your parents probably did, too. Financial guru Dave Ramsey promotes it, and it's easy to see why. It's just easy, period.

The envelope system of budgeting simply involves taking all or most of your cash out of every paycheck and distributing among envelopes that have been earmarked for different things in your budget. For example, you might have an envelope for groceries, one for car expenses, one for utilities, one for eating out, etc. Whatever you plan on spending your money on, give it an envelope. Then, you only spend what is in that envelope, and nothing more. Once the money runs out of one envelope, you can decide whether you want to pull money from another envelope (adjust your budget) or not.

Some apps let you do this virtually, so rather than having actual envelopes, you set up budget categories in the app and 'fund' the budget by telling the app how much you have to spend. You track every purchase and expense in the app so that you can stay within your budget at all times.

Since most people have smartphones, these apps and software programs make it super easy to keep track of your budget anywhere you go, so you don't have any excuse to overspend other than a lack of self-control or emergency, but even emergencies can be dealt with through budgeting for them. (See how awesome budgets are now?)

A few envelope budgeting style apps to try are Betterhaves, Goodbudget Budget Planner, and the MoneyWell app. However, of these three, only Betterhaves is free.

If you want a budgeting app that links to your checking, savings and credit card accounts, you can try the YNAB, which has a software fee, or Mint, which is free. Or, you could just use actual envelopes, you know, the way your parents did.

What's the point?

While the Ultimate Goal of using a budget is to get out of debt and build a substantial fortune for retirement, you should also aim to get at least a month's worth of pay saved up in your checking account, just in case you run into any problems with getting paid in the future. By creating a 'buffer,' you eliminate much of the stress that comes with paying bills. If your boss messes up your paycheck, no problem. Bills still get paid on time, because you're using last month's paycheck to cover them.

It may take a few months before you get entirely comfortable using a budget, but don't give up. Once you start clawing back small amounts of money every month and rolling them into your buffer, you'll start to feel like you just got a pay rise. You'll start feeling in control of your finances, and you might even start to see the light at the end of the tunnel.

Here are your basic budgeting steps again, in case you missed one:

1. Know what you have coming in (paycheck, child support, etc.)
2. Know what you have going out (bills, spending money, etc.)
3. Assign every cent to a particular category (Saving, Rent, Utilities, Kids, etc.)
4. Spend only what you budget for in each category.
5. If you go over in one category, pull from another, and try harder next month!
6. Save up enough to create a one-month buffer in your checking account, just in case…
7. Don't worry if you don't get it right the first month. Just don't give up!

Now that you've wrapped your mind around telling your money what to do, how about we discuss ways to find more of that money to boss around?

Tips, Tricks & Sneaky Ways to Find More Money

You should be really psyched up right about now. You know what you need to do, maybe you've downloaded a few budgeting apps, and you've made your first budget. Good for you, but don't stop there. Remember the title of this book? It's not called Frugal Living for no reason!

When you first start living on a budget, you may only be able to scrape up tiny amounts of 'extra' money for savings. Or, you may find that you don't have enough to meet every budget item every single month. Whatever the reason, you'll want to try and free up as much money as possible to pay off your debt and start building up your savings for a sweet retirement situation.

The Miracle of Saving Money

Now, there is something you should know about saving money. First, it can become highly addictive. Once you start watching your savings account grow, you may never want to touch it, so that you can look at it and see *all the numbers* every time you check your statement. That's okay; it happens to most people.

Second, thanks to the miracle that is compounding interest, even small amounts of savings can be a big deal in ten, twenty or thirty years' time. You may put away a measly $500 in one year, but if you're young and don't spend that money, it could sit and grow in an account for decades, reaching thousands of dollars just by accruing interest on top of interest. Who said savings accounts were boring? Probably someone who was broke…

So, to get started saving that money, after you've worked your budget, use these tips and tricks to help wrangle your money. Some will help you save money, some will help you find money you didn't know you had, and some will help you earn more money with just a little effort.

Pay yourself first

This concept means exactly what it says. Every time you get paid, bill yourself for a certain amount, and pay that 'bill' first. Put the money in your savings account and forget about it. If you don't make your savings a priority, life will find plenty of ways for your money to get frittered away, so establish this habit from the start, even if you're just putting aside $10-15 each time. You have to start somewhere, and the important thing is that you just do it!

You can make this super easy by setting up an automatic transfer to take place every payday, from your checking account to your savings account. This is super easy to set up and is so much better than trying to hide cash in your sock drawer every time you're flush with money because you won't be tempted to spend it.

Check with your bank, because some offer a service that allows you to 'round up' every purchase, moving the difference between the actual cost and the rounded up amount into your savings account. However, don't rely on that type of savings as your only savings method. Paying yourself first is better and smarter, so do that before you do anything else. If it helps, treat it like paying a bill. Just make sure you pay yourself on time, so you don't have to start calling yourself on the phone and asking when you're going to get paid…

Eat more home-cooked foods

If your diet consists mostly of things that come out of a box or a can, your body will thank you for making this change, and your wallet will, too. Research some easy, inexpensive meals that you can cook at home, preferably using basic ingredients that you can use in more than one dish. You don't have to become Betty Crocker or Martha Stewart, but cooking just 3-5 meals a week from 'scratch' can be a lot cheaper and healthier than eating processed foods, fast foods or even restaurant meals.

If you don't have time to cook every day, consider cooking several days' worth of meals one day a week, then freezing or refrigerating them so you'll have them on hand when you need them. You can do this with your lunches for work, too. Just portion out enough for each day and freeze it, then you can pop it in the microwave for a homemade frozen dinner that's far tastier than the ones you buy at the store.

Slow cookers are a frugal person's best friend. You can buy cheaper cuts of meat and cook them all day long, so they'll be nice and tender when you're ready to eat. Plus, you can just toss your ingredients in before you leave for work, then come home to a home-cooked meal with almost no effort.

Stop shopping

Okay, so you can't stop shopping altogether, but you can change the way you shop and the frequency. Grocery spending is one budget category where it's very easy to go over your budget, especially if you are cooking for a family. Start planning your meals, then buying just what you need to prepare those meals. Any other snacks or treats need to be included in the budget or made from scratch using the food you already have.

Stop going to the store 'for one thing.' That is unless you can actually walk into the store, past ten rows of mouthwatering goodies, dazzling gadgets and tempting toys. But, if you're reading this book, you probably can't resist, so just don't do it, or you could end up blowing your budget.

Also, stop viewing shopping as a recreational activity. If you're bored, pick up a book. If you're feeling down, get some exercise. Those endorphins are way better for you than the ones you get from a 'buyer's high' anyway.

Grow your own food

Start a little garden in your backyard, or in a container if you live in an apartment or condo. Grow the vegetables and herbs that you love to eat, and you'll save money on your grocery bill. As a bonus, you'll have an active hobby that can reduce your stress and give you something new to enjoy.

If you do have a little outdoor space, consider growing extra vegetables and selling them to your friends and neighbors. You could end up with a very lucrative side gig during the growing season, and if you have a green thumb, you will never go hungry.

Learn to barter

Do you have skills you can trade in exchange for something else? Maybe you have something that you don't want anymore, and you'd be willing to trade it for something that you do? The barter system is one of the oldest forms of commerce, and although it's not common today, it does still exist.

Websites such as Craigslist and U-Exchange.com are great places to go and barter your time or your stuff for other people's services or stuff. It may not be brand new, but it's new to you, and if you trade wisely, you could end up with better stuff than you had before you were living frugally.

Use coupons and watch for sales

Use this tip with caution! Too many people fall into the habit of chasing a bargain at any cost, which leads to buying stuff they don't need just because it's priced low. Use your coupons and sales wisely. Clip coupons for only the products you'd be buying anyway, and be aware that the item that the coupon is for is almost always more expensive than a generic version, even with the coupon.

You can take advantage of bargains by doing a little comparison shopping every week. Apps like Favado will let you view all the local sales paper for your area on your smartphone so that you can compare prices. You can also clip digital coupons at many retailers' websites for further savings.

<u>Recycle</u>

Recycling is one way that you can save money, make money and help the planet, all at once. If you aren't recycling your scrap metal, such as aluminum cans and empty food tins, you are throwing money away. Most towns have recycling centers that pay for scrap metal, and although it's not much, it can add up if you have a lot of metal to recycle. Copper, brass, and other metals can be recycled too, so scan your home for items and make some extra cash!

Another form of recycling that can save you money is reusing items around your home in different ways. Use old things in new ways to save having to buy new items. Turn boxes and food containers into storage options, turn old clothing into dust cloths or quilts and reuse wrapping paper on gifts to save money and waste.

You can also buy recycled items for less money than buying new ones. An excellent example of this is buying clothing from consignment shops. You can often find nearly-new items for a fraction of the price you'd pay off the rack.

Sell the stuff you don't need

This is how you can find 'hidden' money that you never realized you had. If you take a really good look around your home, you can probably find more than a few items you just don't use anymore. Why let these sit around, taking up space when you could sell them and add to your growing savings?

Have a garage or yard sale to get rid of the things you no longer need or want, and see how much money you can make. You can also sell items online with sites like eBay. You'll be surprised how freeing it can be to turn loose of the 'stuff' that put you into debt in the first place. Your wallet will feel better, and so will you.

DIY

If you own a home or a car, you will have maintenance costs. It's just a given. But, you can minimize those costs by tackling some small jobs yourself. Thanks to the internet, there's literally a video on how to do almost anything in the world, and they're all on YouTube.

Whether you want to tackle some minor

plumbing repairs or build yourself a new set of shelves, there's bound to be a video that walks you through the process so that you can try it for yourself.

Car maintenance is another area where DIY can save you big money. Instead of paying a mechanic $25-60 to change your oil, why not learn how to do that yourself? For the cost of an oil filter and a few quarts of oil, you can do the job at home for far less money.

If you don't have the tools you need, borrow them from a friend or relative, or consider renting them from a hardware store. Be sure that you feel fully comfortable doing your own DIY, or you could cause more damage than good. If you aren't sure what you're doing, ask a friend who may have more experience than you. (Here's another time when bartering may be useful. Barter someone for their services if you can't do it yourself!)

There is more than one way to make sure that your home repairs and auto maintenance get done, and you don't have to pay a fortune for them.

Give handmade gifts

When it comes to being frugal, it can be hard to find gifts that are inexpensive but still meaningful, unless you're willing to get your hands dirty. Handmade gifts are almost always less expensive than store-bought ones, and they come with an added touch of love since you have to make an effort to create them.

Depending on who you are giving gifts to, there are thousands (or more) gift options. You can give homemade food gifts, beauty products, bath soaps, handmade clothing...the possibilities are endless.

You say you don't have any gift-making skills at all, and that your arts and crafts project always look like something the dog dragged in? No worries. YouTube can help with that, too. Also, go to the library, borrow a few books on how to make handcrafted gifts, and let your imagination run wild. Everyone can make *something*, even if it's just a handmade card with a gift certificate that can be redeemed for a little of your time.

Here are a few ideas to get you started:

Food in jars--These are so easy, and inexpensive, that you should be doing these for everyone on your list. There are even eBooks devoted to these food gifts so that you can find inspiration. You put all of the pre-measured dry ingredients needed for a recipe, often a dessert, into a glass jar with a lid. You write the instructions on a piece of paper and attach it to the jar, making sure you indicate whether any other ingredients will be required. Then, you wrap the jar or slap a bow on it, and you have a thoughtful, tasty gift anyone would love to receive.

Scented candles--These can be prohibitively expensive if you buy them in stores, some costing upwards of $20 each. You can make your own with a few supplies from your local arts and crafts store, using essential oils to scent them. The wax used to make candles comes in batches big enough to make several candles so that you could make one for everyone on your gift list, and they'd probably be thrilled.

Knitted scarves--Even if you have never held a pair of knitting needles in your life, you can knit. Knitting looms can be found in most craft stores and are relatively inexpensive. They allow you to wrap yarn around tiny spools set on a frame, then use a small hook to move strands of yarn to perform the 'knitting.' It sounds more complicated than it is; it's actually very easy for a beginner to master. You can get looms of various sizes and shapes so you can make hats, scarves and more.

Of course, you could always rely on your old pal, YouTube, to teach you how to knit the old-fashioned way. Scarves are pretty much one of the simplest things you can make when knitting, and everyone can use a spare scarf.

Of course, you don't have to be crafty to create a great gift for someone. Try making one of these gifts that require absolutely no crafting skills, whatsoever.

Coupon book--Create a book full of coupons that the recipient can redeem for your time or services. You could create coupons for things like a free car wash, a cooked dinner, or a back rub. In fact, you can create coupons for just about anything, so this is perfect for all ages.

Photo book--Do you remember the good old days when people actually printed out photographs and put them in photo albums for others to enjoy? Well, it's time to bring that practice back. Just go through your photos on your phone or camera, print out the best ones and put them in a small photograph album. Give it to someone who will appreciate your artistic endeavors, and enjoy preserving some of those digital photos while making the recipient of your gift happy, too.

Cook a meal--Cook a meal for someone instead of giving them a gift. This can be a great gift to give any time of the year, for friends or family. (For some reason, Moms really like to receive this gift, but only if you wash the dishes afterward, too.)

At the end of the day, it doesn't matter what

type of gift that you give. Just give from the heart, and it's all good. Besides, your recipient probably wouldn't feel great knowing that you overspent on them by buying gifts that blew your budget. If you do want to purchase gifts, be sure to work the cost of the gifts into your budget!

<u>Get involved with the frugal community</u>

Frugal living doesn't have to be a solitary existence. In fact, there are a lot more people enjoying the frugal lifestyle than you might think. Facebook groups, blogs, forums and more exist to help people share their love of frugal living, and there's no better way to pick up new tips and inspiration to keep your eyes on the prize of financial freedom than by talking to others going through the same situation.

It can feel lonely if you are the only one in your circle of family and friends who is trying to live frugally. You may be battling feelings of jealousy, or dealing with people who don't take your efforts to save money seriously. If you don't have someone who understands what you're going through, it could be tempting to throw in the towel and go back to living beyond your means.

Frugal living communities offer more than just support and inspiration. You can generally pick up some really useful ideas that can make your journey a lot easier. Need some frugal recipes, or think you want to try making your household cleaning products, but not sure which websites offer the best advice? Ask your frugal living friends. Chances are, they've tried the things you're not sure about, so they can guide you to the best resources.

To find frugal living communities online, just do a quick web search for 'frugal living communities.' You'll see pages and pages of sites, so you should have no problem finding a place you feel comfortable.

With time and practice, you'll learn all the frugal living tricks and tips, and before you know it, people will be coming to you for advice on saving money. Learn all you can from these communities, because some day, you could end up helping someone you know to become financially independent through frugal living.

Conclusion

Frugal living and getting out of debt aren't outrageous things to do. In fact, just a few generations ago frugality and practicality was embraced and accepted as a part of everyday life. People lived on less than they made and looked forward to a comfortable retirement. Somewhere along the way, our society started embracing debt as a good thing, and so it became as 'natural' as getting married or filing your taxes.

However, debt isn't good. It isn't even natural. Why borrow money for something and pay a ton of interest on that money when you could simply save up for the item and pay cash for it? Why put up with living paycheck to paycheck, stressing about money and wasting time trying to figure out which bill to pay first and hoping you don't have your lights cut off because you 'forgot' to pay your electricity bill again?

By making some small, painless changes and taking control of your money, you are doing more than just living frugally. You are setting yourself up for a future that is bright because you won't have to worry about how you'll fund your lifestyle. Plus, you'll be able to afford to do the things you love when you retire, instead of worrying about money every day.

You will also develop a new sense of self-control, a side-effect of successful budgeting, that will probably spill over into other areas of your life. After all, that dessert or extra drink at the bar looks way less tempting if it threatens to blow your budget.

And, when you reduce the clutter from all the 'stuff' in your life, you make room for more important things, like spending time with your friends and family. You'll become more grateful for the things you have because you'll choose not to surround yourself with 'things' to make you happy. Instead, you'll see these objects for what they really are: just 'stuff' that does not have any bearing on what type of person you really are.

Sure, frugal living will change you, but it will change you for the better. It will awaken a sense of awareness in you that will help you enjoy your life to the fullest. It will also help you to have more money, less stress and fewer worries about your finances. It's definitely a change that's worth making if you want any shot at a happy retirement.

This book won't make these changes for you, but it will hopefully inspire you to dig a little deeper, get yourself on a plan and put that plan to work for your benefit. Who knows, you may be so good at living frugally that you enjoy it more than you ever imagined you could. You could be so good at it that people start asking you for advice, and you'll be able to help them climb out of debt, too.

Once you put this book down, the choice is yours. Choose wisely, or you could end up facing a lifetime of debt followed by a 'retirement' of worry, work, and stress. Financial freedom or anxiety and stress...which will YOU choose?

PAUL MORRISEY

Don't Forget Your Free Gift!

www.EverGreenLearner.com/mybonus

Just visit the link above to download it now.

Thanks!

Paul Morrisey

www.ingramcontent.com/pod-product-compliance
Lightning Source LLC
Chambersburg PA
CBHW070405190526
45169CB00003B/1118